Practice Textbook

CONTENTS

A

Write these numbers in order, starting with the smallest.

1. 6847   7486   6748   8746   7468

2. 4971   1794   1974   4719   4179

3. 8733   3783   3378   3738   3873

B

Make ThHTU numbers from each set of digits.
Write the numbers in order, starting with the largest.

1. 4 7
    9 8

2. 1 5
    2 3

3. 6 5
    9 4

C

After 2981, what is the next number where:
1. the hundreds and tens digits are the same?
2. the hundreds, tens and units digits are the same?
3. the units digit is greater than the hundreds digit?
4. all four digits are the same?

D

What is the value of the purple digit in the following numbers?

1. 2491   2. 3826   3. 4794   4. 9846   5. 1587

6. 3746   7. 8847   8. 3054   9. 6278   10. 5376

A

1. Round each number to the nearest 100.
2. Round each number to the nearest 10.
3. Make each number 10 times bigger.
4. Make each number 100 times bigger.

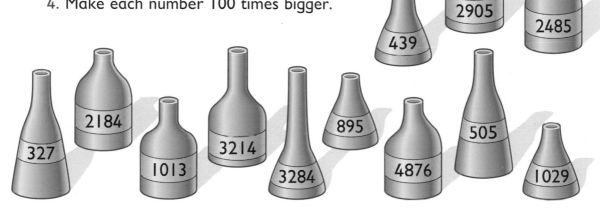

B

Copy and complete the tables for the number machine.

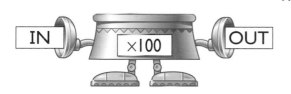

1.

IN	OUT
49	
850	
725	
3164	

2.

IN	OUT
	18 300
	6 200
	20 000
	48 700

C

1. Write the counties in order of size, starting with the smallest.
2. Round the population of each county to the nearest thousand.
   Record your answers.
3. Which county has a population nearest to 90 000?
4. Which county has a population nearest to 40 000?

Counties of Ireland	
County	Population
Carlow	39820
Clare	87567
Kilkenny	70806
Longford	31140
Louth	88514
Sligo	55474
Wicklow	87449

A Add each of these numbers to 9999.
Write your answers.

1. 1	2. 6	3. 14	4. 27
5. 84	6. 100	7. 125	8. 199

B Write the value of the purple digit.

1. 59 428   2. 37 296   3. 21 147   4. 98 164
5. 31 049   6. 88 147   7. 38 915   8. 29 976

C Write each list of numbers in order, starting with the smallest.

1.	49 128	48 219	29 481	84 921	48 129
2.	37 146	36 417	46 137	73 164	37 614
3.	21 480	41 082	42 801	41 280	41 208

D 1. Write the distances in order, starting with the largest.
2. Round these distances to the nearest 100 km.

Distances in km
London ←14 466→ Perth
Rome ←10 212→ Los Angeles
Paris ←16 959→ Sydney
Madrid ←19 592→ Auckland
Berlin ←11 890→ Buenos Aires
Amsterdam ←16 544→ Melbourne

E Make ThHTU numbers for each set of digits.
Write the numbers in order, starting with the smallest.

1. 7 1
    4 9

2. 6 3
    2 7

3. 0 6
    9 4

4. 3 0
    5 5

5. 8 5
    1 9

6. 5 2
    4 8

A Write these numbers in figures.

1. Sixty thousand four hundred and seventy-eight.
2. Twenty-five thousand two hundred and ninety-four.
3. Four hundred and ten thousand three hundred and six.
4. Eight hundred and thirty-five thousand one hundred and twenty-nine.
5. Nine hundred and seven thousand four hundred and sixty-four.

 B Write these numbers in words.

1. 72 499   2. 846 304   3. 780 461   4. 821 093

 C Write the value of the purple digit.

1. 930 467   2. 230 000   3. 492 196   4. 711 836

5. 833 004   6. 680 291   7. 522 263   8. 141 638

D

1. Write the regions in order of size, starting with the smallest.
2. Round the population of each region to the nearest thousand.

Regions of Scotland	
Region	Population
Central	272 077
Fife	344 590
Grampion	502 863
Highland	200 608
Lothian	743 766
Tayside	393 498

 E Subtract 999 from each of these numbers.

1. 15 426   2. 7946   3. 24 717   4. 9744
5. 16 304   6. 2999   7. 30 429   8. 47 648

A Write the shaded part of each shape as a decimal.

1. 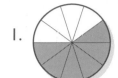   2.   3.   4.

5. 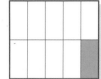   6.   7. 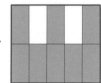   8.

 B Write each group of decimals in order of size, starting with the smallest.

1. 0.6 0.4 0.9 0.7
   0.1 0.3 0.5

2. 1.3 1.8 0.9 1.4
   1.1 1.9 1.6

3. 4.2 5.6 3.9 4.6
   3.7 4.1 4.8

4. 17.9 18.4 18.9 17.6
   18.1 16.7 19.3

C Write each point marked by a letter as a decimal.

1.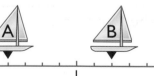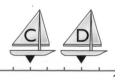

0   1   2   3

2.

0   1   2   3   4   5   6

3.

0   1

A Rearrange each of these sets to make a number as near as possible to 7.

 1. 5 7 •

 2. 9 • 6

 3. • 5 8

 4. 9 4 •

5. • 2 8

6. 6 7 •

B

1. Write the numbers in order, starting with the smallest.
2. Round each number to the nearest whole number.

2.1   0.8   1.9   1.4   0.6   2.8

C

Match the decimal numbers shown to A, B and C.

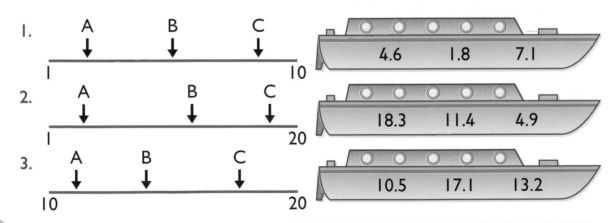

1.
   A   B   C
   ↓   ↓   ↓
   1_____10

   4.6   1.8   7.1

2.
   A   B   C
   ↓   ↓   ↓
   1_____20

   18.3   11.4   4.9

3.
   A   B   C
   ↓   ↓   ↓
   10_____20

   10.5   17.1   13.2

D Round each of these numbers to the nearest whole number.

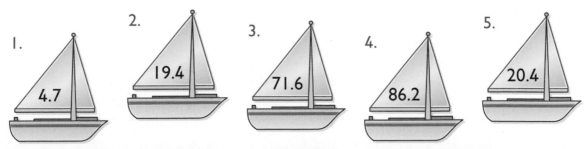

1. 4.7
2. 19.4
3. 71.6
4. 86.2
5. 20.4

A Write these fractions as decimals.

1. $\frac{6}{10}$　　　2. $\frac{4}{10}$　　　3. $\frac{7}{10}$　　　4. $\frac{9}{10}$　　　5. $\frac{3}{10}$

6. $\frac{28}{100}$　　　7. $\frac{92}{100}$　　　8. $\frac{36}{100}$　　　9. $\frac{17}{100}$　　　10. $\frac{8}{100}$

B Write (then add) the numbers in each chain in order of size, starting with the smallest.

1. 2.14 | 3.92 | 2.46 | 2.18 | 3.29 | 2.08

2. 3.61 | 2.99 | 3.09 | 4.14 | 2.90 | 3.16

3. 4.8 | 5.21 | 4.96 | 4.83 | 4.08 | 4.9

C Write out each statement, adding >, < or = to make the statement true.

1. 1·04 ☐ 1·4　　　2. 6·2 ☐ 6·12　　　3. 12·4 ☐ 1·24

4. 17·19 ☐ 17·06　　　5. 4·9 ☐ 4·90　　　6. 8·21 ☐ 8·3

D Write the next three numbers in each list.

1. 0.43　　0.44　　0.45　　_____　_____　_____

2. 6.06　　6.07　　6.08　　_____　_____　_____

3. 19.55　　19.54　　19.53　　_____　_____　_____

4. 2.96　　2.97　　2.98　　_____　_____　_____

A

These are the finishing times in a 200 metre race.

| 21.58 sec | 20.09 sec | 21.20 sec | 20.72 sec | 21.02 sec | 20.27 sec | 20.40 sec | 21.19 sec |

1. Which athlete won the race?
2. Who came third?
3. Who finished 1·1 seconds behind the winner?
4. Write the times in order, starting with the winner.
5. Write each time to the nearest whole number.

B

Round each of these to the nearest whole number.

1. 43.55
2. 9.97
3. 12.04
4. 24.61
5. 28.49
6. 8.09
7. 35.29
8. 54.72

C

Rearrange these sets to make a number as near as possible to 5.

1. 4 . 6 5

2. 3 2 . 7

3. 2 9 4 .

4. 8 9 3 .

5. 5 . 7 4

6. 2 8 . 1

A

Copy and complete the sums.

1. 4 9 2 1
  + 3 0 6 5
  _____

2. 8 3 1 5
  + 1 5 6 2
  _____

3. 4 8 2 9
  + 3 1 5 2
  _____

4. 6 2 1 7
  + 1 3 4 8
  _____

5. 6 2 5 4
  + 2 1 8 6
  _____

6. 4 2 2 9
  + 2 7 9 3
  _____

7. 4 7 1 8
  + 3 2 9 2
  _____

8. 3 9 0 5
  + 5 2 8 5
  _____

B

These are the number of words in each book.

3468 2944 4063 2919 3824 4787

Write the following totals.

1. The first two books.
2. The fifth and sixth books.
3. The middle two books.
4. The first and last books.
5. The first three books.
6. The last three books.

C

Add 1998 to each of these.

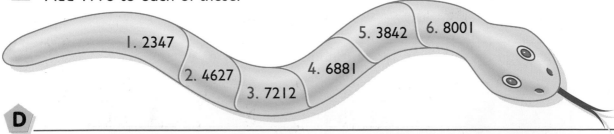

1. 2347
2. 4627
3. 7212
4. 6881
5. 3842
6. 8001

D

Sort these numbers into pairs that add up to 5000. Write your answers.

1.
1348
2428   189
4811
1563
2572
3437
3652

2.
4067   1188
       3812   871
2994
       4129
933   2006

A Total these.

1. 3418 + 3581

2. 3451 + 2548

3. 4255 + 4744

4. 3256 + 4743

5. 2787 + 4211

6. 2399 + 2600

B

Write your answers to these questions.

1. What is the total of the even numbers?
2. What is the total of the odd numbers?
3. Which two numbers give the largest total?
4. Which three numbers give a total of 9999?

1729   4837   5944   3781   2326

C

Copy and complete the sums.

1.
```
    4 6 1 ◌
  + 3 ◌4 8
  ◌8 6 7
```

2.
```
    1 8 4 9
  + ◌6 6 ◌
    5 5 ◌3
```

3.
```
    2 9 ◌5
  + 5 ◌1 ◌
  ◌5 3 1
```

4.
```
    4 ◌9 4
  + ◌7 ◌6
    8 0 8 ◌
```

D

The number in each circle is the total of two consecutive numbers.
Write the sums.

1.  6945

[ ] + [ ]

2.  5691

[ ] + [ ]

3.  9333

[ ] + [ ]

4.  4837

[ ] + [ ]

A Find the totals of these sums.

1. 4831 + 2958 + 1372
2. 1069 + 3428 + 2187
3. 2199 + 1480 + 679
4. 497 + 3184 + 2805

B Copy and complete these grids.

Add each row. Add each column. Find the grand total.

1.

1381	3184	
2962	1871	

2.

2811	2448	
3789	1037	

3.

2688	3914	
1002	1892	

C These fish tanks hold different amounts of water.

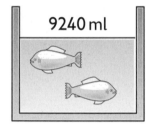
9240 ml

6480 ml

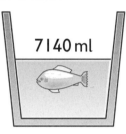
7140 ml

8630 ml

Write the totals of these.

1. 9240 ml + 6480 ml
2. 7140 ml + 8630 ml
3. 9240 ml + 8630 ml
4. 6480 ml + 7140 ml + 8630 ml
5. 9240 ml + 6480 ml + 7140 ml + 8630 ml

D Add 9876 to each of these.

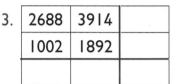

2. 2837

3. 1921

4. 3848

5. 2998

1. 1341

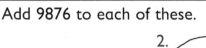

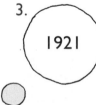

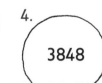

6. 3249

A Add up the prices and write your answers.

1. Car A and car C   2. Car D and car E   3. Car B and car A
4. Car C, car D and car B.   5. The total of all the cars

B This chart shows how far a car travelled each year.

year	1	2	3	4	5
kilometres travelled	8249	7152	9183	6298	8498

1. What was the total distance in years 3 and 4?
2. What was the total distance in years 2 and 3?
3. Were more kilometres travelled in years 1 and 2 or years 4 and 5?
4. What was the total number of kilometres travelled?

C Write the pairs which add to 8000.

A Copy and complete these sums.

1.	3 9 2 8 − 2 1 1 7	2.	4 6 1 4 − 3 1 0 2	3.	7 2 1 8 − 3 1 3 7	4.	8 2 7 6 − 4 1 5 7
5.	4 8 4 5 − 2 1 5 9	6.	3 1 0 6 − 1 9 2 5	7.	2 9 1 4 − 1 5 9 9	8.	9 3 0 5 − 2 4 6 6

B Write the differences between each of these pairs.

1.	2.	3.	4.	5.
2147 3924	6829 8019	4164 5007	7204 3827	7306 4209

C

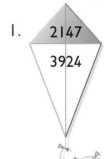

1. Write down how many of each type of sweet have been sold.
2. Which sweet sold the most?
3. Which sweet sold the least?
4. Which sweet sold about 3000?

Sweet	Number of sweets in stock		Number of sweets sold
	Monday	Friday	
Cola cube	2147	1628	
Sugar surprise	4243	2915	
Pear drop	3194	1826	
Candy crunch	4856	1947	
Nut cluster	2894	1637	

A Subtract each of these numbers from 3000.

1.
1684

2.
794

3.
1837

4.
2168

B Subtract each of these numbers from 6000.

1.
4845

2.
3992

3.
5240

4.
4711

C How much farther is it from London to Cape Town than from London to:

1. Delhi?
2. Tokyo?
3. Nairobi?
4. Montreal?
5. Los Angeles?

Distances from London in km

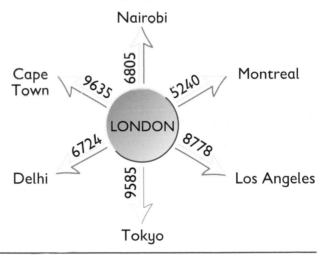

D Write the answers to these sums.

1. 6724 – 5240
2. 6805 – 6724
3. 9585 – 8778
4. 8778 – 6805
5. 9585 – 5240
6. 6805 – 5240

E Find the missing digits.
Copy and complete the sums.

1.
```
    3 8 4 ☆
  - 1 7 ☆ 2
    2 ☆ 8 5
```

2.
```
    7 ☆ 4 3
  - 2 4 8 ☆
  ☆ 4 5 7
```

3.
```
    4 1 1 5
  - 2 ☆ 3 ☆
  ☆ 1 7 9
```

4.
```
    5 2 ☆ 0
  - ☆ 1 9 6
    2 0 9 ☆
```

A

Complete these sums.

1. 9847 – 3729   2. 8427 – 1984   3. 6299 – 4089
4. 7003 – 2918   5. 3240 – 1086   6. 9417 – 7298

B

Sort these numbers into pairs that have a difference of 1299.
Write your answers.

1083   2495   1848   2382   3299   3147   2000   1196

C

Write your answers to the following questions.

1. What is the difference in weight between the heaviest and lightest parcels?
2. What is the difference in weight between parcels A and C?
3. Which two parcels have a difference of 2031g?

A   3245 g   B   1841 g   C   2915 g

D   2172 g   E   6891 g   F   4203 g

D

Copy and answer the sums.
Find the odd one out.

| 1. | 7 8 4 6
– 6 6 1 2 | 2. | 4 2 1 1
– 2 9 7 7 | 3. | 5 1 0 6
– 3 8 7 2 | 4. | 8 3 9 1
– 7 1 5 7 |

| 5. | 2 0 0 1
–   7 6 7 | 6. | 3 0 7 2
– 1 8 3 8 | 7. | 6 7 0 2
– 5 3 7 8 | 8. | 8 5 3 2
– 7 2 9 8 |

Write how much change there is from £10 for each of these.

1. £4.28   2. £8.30   3. £6.72   4. £9.36

5. £8.04   6. £1.21   7. £3.33   8. £5.08

B

Write the difference in price between the following pairs of items.

1. A and C   2. D and B   3. G and F   4. E and H

A
£14.29

B
£16.73

C
£9.50

D
£12.45

E
£12.05

F
£8.70

G
£13.84

H
£19.40

Write the pairs of items that have the following price differences.

5. £2.24   6. £10·70   7. £2·89   8. £2·95

C

These are the results of a shopping survey.

Item	Most expensive price found	Least expensive price found
Dartboard	£21·45	£13·80
Remote-control car	£49·50	£12·55
Walkie talkie	£37·99	£16·84
Rucksack	£38·35	£8·90
Rollerskates	£44·85	£17·21
Torch	£21·05	£3·81

Write the difference between the least
and most expensive price for each item.

This table shows what was sold in a gift shop.

Item	Jan.	Feb.	Mar.	Total (Approx)
Bangles	4163	2970	1465	
Jigsaws	2140	3567	2452	
Keyrings	4024	1529	2646	
Pencils	3928	4210	1358	
Postcards	1451	2305	1948	
Posters	2042	3194	2009	

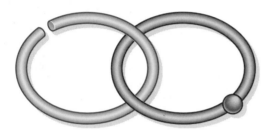

1. Copy the table, rounding each number to the nearest 100.
2. Write the approximate total sales for each item.

B

1. Round each of these numbers to the nearest 1000.
2. Sort the numbers into pairs that total approximately 8000.

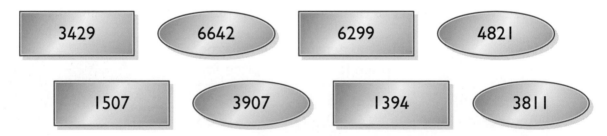

| 3429 | 6642 | 6299 | 4821 |

| 1507 | 3907 | 1394 | 3811 |

C

Round each number to the nearest 100.

1. 4925 – 3852
2. 5198 – 2924
3. 6248 – 978
4. 2883 – 1424
5. 9809 – 6192
6. 8229 – 4747

Complete the sums using these new numbers.

This table shows the litres of petrol sold in one day at a petrol station.

Day	Morning	Afternoon	Approximate difference
Monday	5815	4293	
Tuesday	4711	5944	
Wednesday	6209	3875	
Thursday	3795	4248	
Friday	5154	3249	
Saturday	4485	4208	

1. Copy the table, rounding each number to the nearest 100.
2. Write the approximate difference between the morning and afternoon sales for each day.
3. On which days were the most and the least petrol sold?

B

1. Round each of these numbers to the nearest 1000.
2. Sort the numbers into pairs with a difference of approximately 3000.

9483   4285   5609   6804   3339   5725   4218   972

C

Round the numbers in each sum to the nearest 100.
Now write the approximate answers.
1. 2147 + 3829 + 1821
2. 6852 + 2049
3. 2199 + 3698
4. 2409 + 6237
5. 2409 + 2852 + 1247
6. 1152 + 6103 + 2949

A This table shows attendance figures at a transport museum.

1. How many people visited the museum in July and August?
2. What was the difference between the highest and lowest number of visitors?
3. How many visitors were there in May, June and October?
4. Round each number to the nearest 100. What was the approximate total number of visitors?

Month	Number of visitors
April	3871
May	4294
June	7840
July	6218
August	8547
September	5308
October	4952

B
1. From 8391 subtract 3719.
2. What is the difference between 3846 and 7219?
3. Which number is 2948 less than 6149?
4. What is 2842 minus 1359?

C
1. The difference between two numbers is 1649.
   The smaller number is 3685.
   What is the other number?

2. The difference between two numbers is 3204.
   The smaller number is 2543.
   What is the larger number?

3. The difference between two numbers is 2312.
   The larger number is 9850.
   What is the smaller number?

4. The difference between two numbers is 1849.
   If one number is 6022 what could the other number be?

A

These are the numbers of tins of paint in each colour at a DIY superstore.

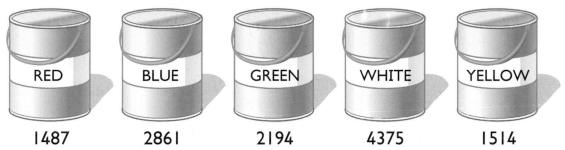

RED	BLUE	GREEN	WHITE	YELLOW
1487	2861	2194	4375	1514

1. What is the difference between the number of tins of yellow and the number of tins of blue?
2. What is the total number of tins of green, white and red?
3. How many more tins of white than green are there?
4. Which two colours, when added together, equal the number of tins of white paint?

B

1. Two of these numbers are needed to open the safe.
   They have a sum of 7253 and a difference of 825.
   What are the two numbers?
2. Which two numbers total 8156?
3. Which number is 1563 less than 4214?

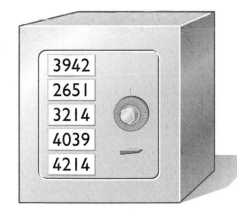

3942
2651
3214
4039
4214

C

1. The difference between two numbers is 4785.
   The larger number is 9837.
   What is the other number?

2. The difference between two numbers is 2189.
   The smaller number is 1702.
   What is the larger number?

A

Do these as quickly as you can. Write the answers.

1.
4×9
3×7
6×2
8×8
3×5
10×7

2.
8×4
6×5
9×2
7×7
3×6
4×7

3.
7×2
3×9
5×4
10×6
8×4
6×7

B

Write what each machine does.

1.
6 → 42
2 → 14
4 → 28
8 → 56

2.
8 → 32
3 → 12
9 → 36
5 → 20

3.
6 → 48
8 → 64
9 → 72
4 → 32

C

Copy and complete these sums.

1. $4 \times$ $= 24$ 2. $8 \times$ 🧁 $= 56$ 3. 🧁 $\times 4 = 36$ 4. 🧁 $\times 6 = 30$

5. $3 \times$ 🧁 $= 27$ 6. 🧁 $\times 5 = 35$ 7. $6 \times$ 🧁 $= 18$ 8. 🧁 $\times 9 = 18$

D

1. Multiply each of these numbers by 6.

| 7 | 4 | 3 | 8 | 9 | 6 |

2. Multiply each of these numbers by 9.

| 3 | 9 | 4 | 8 | 7 | 6 |

E

Copy and complete these tables.

×	4	5	6	7	8
4					
6					
8					

×	4	5	6	7	8
5					
7					
9					

A Do these as quickly as you can. Write the answers.

1.
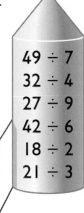
49 ÷ 7
32 ÷ 4
27 ÷ 9
42 ÷ 6
18 ÷ 2
21 ÷ 3

2.
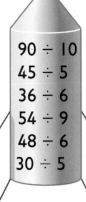
90 ÷ 10
45 ÷ 5
36 ÷ 6
54 ÷ 9
48 ÷ 6
30 ÷ 5

3.
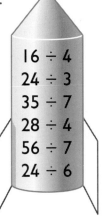
16 ÷ 4
24 ÷ 3
35 ÷ 7
28 ÷ 4
56 ÷ 7
24 ÷ 6

B Copy and complete these sums.

1.
▢ ÷ 6
▢ ÷ 8
▢ ÷ 9   6
▢ ÷ 4

2.
▢ ÷ 5
▢ ÷ 7
▢ ÷ 3   4
▢ ÷ 9

3.
▢ ÷ 7
▢ ÷ 9
▢ ÷ 4   7
▢ ÷ 8

C Write what each machine does.

1.

18   3
30   5
48   8
36   6

2.
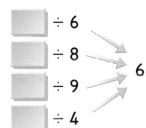
28   7
36   9
24   6
16   4

3.
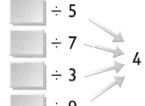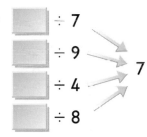
64   8
32   4
72   9
24   3

D 1. Write the numbers that can be divided exactly by 8.

14   72   34   24   18
80   63   42
32   36   48   16

2. Write the numbers that can be divided exactly by 7.

49   27   42   21   17
34   35   12
32   28   70   14

A Work out and write the answers as quickly as you can.

1.
24 ÷ 6
81 ÷ 9
35 ÷ 7
18 ÷ 3
72 ÷ 8
25 ÷ 5

2.
3 × 9
4 × 7
6 × 2
5 × 9
8 × 3
7 × 10

3.
90 ÷ 9
15 ÷ 3
28 ÷ 7
63 ÷ 9
42 ÷ 7
27 ÷ 3

4.
4 × 9
8 × 2
3 × 7
5 × 6
8 × 8
7 × 7

B Write what comes out of each machine.

1.
IN   OUT
3   ?
9   ?
2   ?
7   ?

× 6

2.
IN   OUT
16   ?
24   ?
36   ?
28   ?

÷ 4

3.
IN   OUT
4   ?
8   ?
7   ?
6   ?

× 9

C Write the answers.
Find the odd one out.

1. (30 ÷ 5)   2. (6 × 4)   3. (9 × 3)

4. (64 ÷ 8)   5. (42 ÷ 7)   6. (4 × 8)   7. (90 ÷ 9)   8. (7 × 6)

D

1. Divide each number by 6.
   Write the answers.

   36   12   18   48   30   24

2. Divide each number by 7.
   Write the answers.

   49   14   35   70   42   21

E Copy and complete these number patterns.

1. 7, 14, 21, __ __ __ __

2. __ __ 18, 24, __ 36, __

3. __ __ __ 16, __ 24, 28

4. __ 18, __ __ __ 54, 63

A

Do these as quickly as you can. Write the answers.

1.

8×3
9×4
3×7
4×2
6×6
5×4

2.

$18 \div 6$
$72 \div 9$
$24 \div 6$
$32 \div 8$
$16 \div 4$
$25 \div 5$

3.

10×6
8×4
6×5
9×7
6×8
4×3

4.

$27 \div 9$
$30 \div 6$
$49 \div 7$
$28 \div 4$
$64 \div 8$
$90 \div 10$

B

Copy and complete the tables.

1.

×	6	3	8
2	12		
5			
9			

2.

×	9		
4		24	
	45		
7			14

3.

×			
	25		
		49	
			81

C

Copy and complete.

1.

2.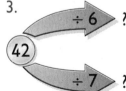

3.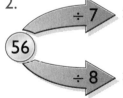

4.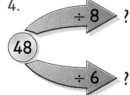

D

Copy and complete.

1. $8 \times \clubsuit = 56$ 2. $6 \times \clubsuit = 24$ 3. $4 \times \clubsuit = 28$ 4. $7 \times \clubsuit = 63$

5. $\clubsuit \times 3 = 27$ 6. $\clubsuit \times 7 = 35$ 7. $\clubsuit \times 9 = 36$ 8. $\clubsuit \times 5 = 40$

E

Copy and complete.

1. $\heartsuit \div 3 = 7$ 2. $\heartsuit \div 6 = 9$ 3. $\heartsuit \div 7 = 7$ 4. $\heartsuit \div 5 = 3$

5. $24 \div \heartsuit = 6$ 6. $72 \div \heartsuit = 8$ 7. $54 \div \heartsuit = 9$ 8. $63 \div \heartsuit = 7$

A Copy and complete these sums.

1. 7 3
    × __4__
    ‾‾‾

2. 8 6
    × __5__
    ‾‾‾

3. 3 9
    × __6__
    ‾‾‾

4. 6 4
    × __9__
    ‾‾‾

5. 5 1
    × __8__
    ‾‾‾

B Write the cost of the following items.

 27p

 32p

 49p

 38p

 63p

 59p

1. six pens   2. eight chocolate bars   3. four note pads   4. nine erasers
5. eight magazines 6. five postcards   7. seven erasers   8. eight pens

C Write which answer is nearest to 500.

1. (88 × 9)   2. (67 × 8)   3. (92 × 6)   4. (63 × 9)   5. (73 × 7)

D Find the missing digits.
Copy and complete the sums.

1.   7 ●
    × ____6
    ‾‾‾‾‾
      4 5 0

2.   ● 4
    × ____9
    ‾‾‾‾‾
      7 5 6

3.   3 8
    × ____●
    ‾‾‾‾‾
      1 5 2

4.   9 ●
    × ____6
    ‾‾‾‾‾
      5 4 6

5.   ● 8
    × ____8
    ‾‾‾‾‾
      2 2 ●

E Sort these numbers into pairs where one number is double the other.

48   184   56   81   92   28
46   162   96   23   158   79

A How many stamps are in each of these albums?

1.  128 pages

 6 stamps on each page.

2. 245 pages

 5 stamps on each page.

3. 289 pages

8 stamps on each page.

4. 226 pages

9 stamps on each page.

B Copy and complete these sums.

1.	2 5 9	2.	1 8 9	3.	3 8 2	4.	2 1 7	5.	4 0 9
×	5	×	4	×	7	×	6	×	8

C Write the answer that is nearest to 2000.

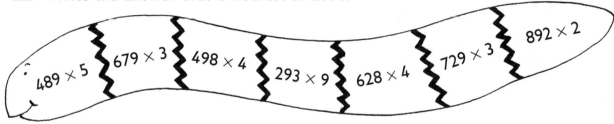

489×5 679×3 498×4 293×9 628×4 729×3 892×2

D Write the total number of each sweet.

1.  138 138 138

2. 240 240 240 240

3. 325 325 325 325 325 325

4.  296 296 296 296 296

5.    525 525 525 525

A

Copy and complete these sums.

1.	2 8 7	2.	3 9 5	3.	8 2 1	4.	6 2 9	5.	8 4 6
	× 4		× 6		× 7		× 3		× 5

B

There are 345 sheets of paper in one pack.
How many sheets are there in:

1. two packs?   2. four packs?   3. five packs?   4. nine packs?

C

Write your answers to these sums.
Which is the odd one out?

1. 644 × 7   2. 836 × 3   3. 854 × 2

4. 476 × 8   5. 512 × 4   6. 368 × 6

D

Copy and complete this table.

Pins in a box	Number of boxes	Total number of pins
440	6	
252	7	
384	5	
192	6	
308	8	

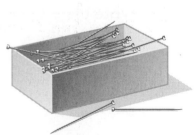

E

Which answer is bigger in each of these pairs:

1. 998 × 8   or   889 × 9 ?   2. 404 × 5   or   505 × 4 ?

3. 987 × 6   or   678 × 9 ?   4. 363 × 6   or   636 × 3 ?

Make each of these numbers eight times bigger.
Write the answers.

1. 426

2. 354

3. 291

4. 607

5. 349

6. 729

B

Write your answers to these sums.
Which answer is nearest to 5000?

1. 747×7 2. 826×6 3. 996×5 4. 651×8 5. 718×7 6. 591×9

C

This machine can make 245 pins in one minute.
How many pins are made in:

1. three minutes?   2. five minutes?

3. seven minutes?   4. eight minutes?

D

There are 380 pins in each box.
How many pins are there in:

1. seven boxes?   2. four boxes?

3. nine boxes?   4. six boxes?

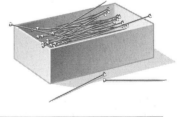

E

Find the missing digits.
Copy and complete the sums.

1.
```
   2 ▲ 9
 ×     6
 1 6 7 4
```

2.
```
   4 8 ▲
 ×     5
 ▲ 4 1 0
```

3.
```
   ▲ 0 9
 ×     7
 4 9 6 ▲
```

4.
```
   ▲ 9 4
 ×     8
 3 1 ▲ 2
```

5.
```
   5 6 ▲
 ×     4
 ▲ 2 4 0
```

A

Copy and complete these sums.

1. 6⟌74   2. 5⟌95   3. 8⟌96   4. 4⟌78

5. 7⟌91   6. 4⟌63   7. 3⟌79   8. 6⟌84

B

Write the answers to these sums.
Which is the odd one out?

1.
$49 \div 4$

2.
$55 \div 6$

3.
$37 \div 3$

4.
$86 \div 6$

5.
$96 \div 5$

6.
$93 \div 4$

C

1. Divide each of these numbers by 4.
Write your answers.   53   78   95   67

2. Divide each of these numbers by 5.
Write your answers.   77   69   91   83

3. Divide each of these numbers by 6.
Write your answers.   75   94   85   69

D

Which numbers cannot be
divided exactly by 3?

91   54   70

74

44   69   48   86

E

Find the missing digits.
Copy and complete the sums.

```
      △1r4              13            △3r△            3△r1
1. 7⟌81          2. 6⟌7△          3. 4⟌95          4. 3⟌△7

      1△r1            11r3            △r△            19r△
5. 5⟌76          6. 8⟌9△          7. 9⟌87          8. 4⟌△8
```

A

Jill has the following plants.
She has six tubs to fill.
How many of each plant
can she put in each of her tubs?
Write your answers.

Pansies	168
Lobelias	150
Cornflowers	204
Marigolds	186
Geraniums	162
Poppies	228

B

Copy and complete these sums.

1. 7)497   2. 5)645   3. 9)630   4. 3)435

5. 8)392   6. 7)504   7. 4)392   8. 5)905

C

Answer these sums.
Write which is the odd one out.

1.  483 ÷ 7   2.  472 ÷ 8   3. 534 ÷ 6   4. 441 ÷ 9

5. 476 ÷ 7   6. 195 ÷ 5   7.  356 ÷ 4   8.  792 ÷ 8

D

The buns, biscuits and cakes are
shared equally into eight boxes.
Write how many buns, biscuits
and cakes are in each box.

CAKES 504   BISCUITS 296   BUNS 424

E

Find the missing digits.
Copy and complete these sums.

1.   △5
   5)375

2.   48
   7)△36

3.   73
   4)2△2

4.   △8
   9)612

5.   28△
   3)840

6.   96
   6)5△6

7.   11△
   8)920

8.   1△2
   4)728

Copy and complete these sums.

1. 7⟌328   2. 4⟌692   3. 5⟌927   4. 3⟌824

5. 6⟌594   6. 8⟌327   7. 9⟌907   8. 4⟌920

 B

Balloons are tied in groups of five, write how many groups can be made, and the remainders from the following:

1. 147 balloons   2. 109 balloons   3. 211 balloons
4. 318 balloons   5. 225 balloons   6. 193 balloons

C

Divide each of these numbers by 9.
Write the answers.

1.  624   2.  904   3.  836   4.  671   5.  408

6.  177   7.  349   8.  455   9.  327   10.  412

 D

Write the remainders of these sums.

1. 318 ÷ 9   2. 275 ÷ 6   3. 137 ÷ 5   4. 309 ÷ 8
5. 865 ÷ 7   6. 892 ÷ 6   7. 553 ÷ 4   8. 919 ÷ 3

E

Find the missing digits.
Copy and complete the sums.

         208r1   65r3   98r3   136r5   301r2   111r7
1. 4⟌83△   2. 6⟌39△   3. 5⟌49△   4. 7⟌95△   5. 3⟌90△   6. 8⟌89△

         124r2   84r7   129r2   46r4   87r3   72r2
7. 3⟌37△   8. 9⟌76△   9. 4⟌51△   10. 5⟌23△   11. 8⟌69△   12. 6⟌43△

A

Write down which of these sums has a remainder of 4.

1. 852 ÷ 3

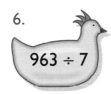
2. 658 ÷ 5

3. 796 ÷ 6

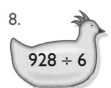
4. 893 ÷ 7

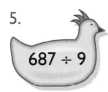
5. 687 ÷ 9

6. 963 ÷ 7

7. 337 ÷ 5

8. 928 ÷ 6

B

Write which of these numbers:

677   780   116   425   762

1. divide exactly by 5;
2. divide exactly by 6;
3. have a remainder of 1 when divided by 4;
4. have a remainder of 2 when divided by 3.

C

Copy and complete these sums.
Put a ring around the odd one out.

1. 6 ⟌ 350
2. 7 ⟌ 863
3. 8 ⟌ 554
4. 3 ⟌ 749

5. 9 ⟌ 650
6. 4 ⟌ 830
7. 5 ⟌ 753
8. 3 ⟌ 731

D

An egg box holds six eggs.
How many egg boxes are needed to hold:

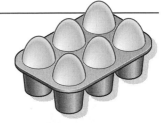

1. 204 eggs?
2. 627 eggs?
3. 423 eggs?
4. 195 eggs?
5. 314 eggs?
6. 572 eggs?

E

Divide each of these numbers by 8.

1. 647
2. 837
3. 557
4. 903
5. 854
6. 906
7. 735
8. 589

A

1. Which of these numbers can be divided equally by 4?
2. Which number equals 81 × 6?
3. Find the number which is three times bigger than another of these numbers.
4. Which number is nearest to 2000 when it is multiplied by 5?

385   176   486

304   272   528

B

Write the answers to these sums.
Which is the odd one out?

1. 384 × 4
2.  952 ÷ 7
3.  288 ÷ 8
4.  324 ÷ 9

5. 406 × 6
6. 544 ÷ 4
7. 274 × 9

C

Do these sums in your head. Write the answers.

1. 250 × 3   2. 124 × 2   3. 105 × 5   4. 333 × 2
5. 120 × 4   6. 750 × 2   7. 502 × 3   8. 800 × 6

D

Do these sums in your head. Write the answers.

1. 500 ÷ 2   2. 240 ÷ 3   3. 150 ÷ 5   4. 360 ÷ 6
5. 640 ÷ 8   6. 700 ÷ 2   7. 880 ÷ 4   8. 140 ÷ 7

E

Do these sums in your head. Write the answers.

1. 736 × 5   2. 425 × 3   3. 624 × 4   4. 109 × 8
5. 374 ÷ 6   6. 847 ÷ 5   7. 924 ÷ 4   8. 523 ÷ 7

A Look at the numbers which are opposite each other.
Write the missing numbers.

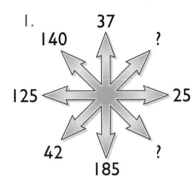
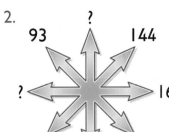
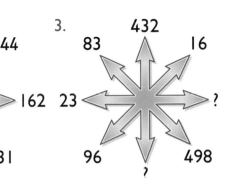

1.
37
140 ?
125 ← → 25
42 ?
185

2.
?
93 144
? ← → 162
48 31
72

3.
432
83 16
23 ← → ?
96 498
?

B Write which of these gives:

1. the smallest answer;   2. the largest answer.

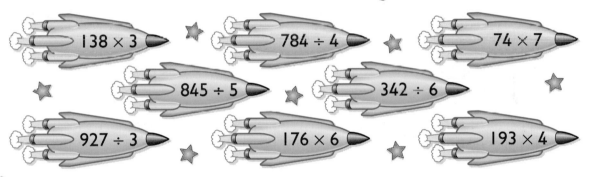

138 × 3   784 ÷ 4   74 × 7

845 ÷ 5   342 ÷ 6

927 ÷ 3   176 × 6   193 × 4

C Write the answers to these.
Find the pairs that total 2000.

1. 371 × 3   2. 960 ÷ 5   3. 888 ÷ 6   4. 221 × 4
5. 463 × 4   6. 976 ÷ 4   7. 452 × 4   8. 878 × 2

D Answer each sum.

1. 121 × 5   2. 901 × 4   3. 890 ÷ 5   4. 341 × 6   5. 888 ÷ 3
6. 848 ÷ 8   7. 781 × 5   8. 684 ÷ 4   9. 499 × 6   10. 812 ÷ 2

Use the code breaker to change each of your digits to a letter.
What word does each answer make?

0	1	2	3	4	5	6	7	8	9
A	B	D	S	R	P	T	I	N	O

A

Write the cost of the following.

1. six tubes of toothpaste
2. four bottles of shampoo
3. eight sponges
4. three handcreams
5. five tubs of hair gel

 B

How much money is saved by buying:

1. a pack of three toothbrushes instead of three single toothbrushes?
2. a pack of three soaps instead of three single soaps?
3. the five toothpaste pack instead of five single toothpastes?

 C

How much change from £20 would you get for each of these shopping lists:

1.
two hair gels

three shampoos

two sponges

2.
three
toothpastes

two packs of
three soaps

four handcreams

3.
four shampoos

three sponges

two soaps

A Write your answers to these questions.

1. Which number is eight times greater than 450?
2. How many sixes are there in 828?
3. What is $\frac{1}{4}$ of 152?
4. What is the product of 218 and 4?

B

1. One book costs £4·75.
   What would seven books cost?

2. One box weighs 852 g.
   What would six boxes weigh?

3. 1m of fabric costs £2·72.
   What would 8 m cost?

4. One bottle holds 685 ml.
   What would five bottles hold?

5. One lap of a track is 400 m.
   What is ten laps of the track?

6. 1 kg of dog food costs £3·04.
   What would 7 kg cost?

C

1. A lorry can carry 348 crates.
   How many crates can it carry
   in eight loads?

2. A length of wood 238 cm long is cut
   into seven equal pieces.
   How long is each piece of wood?

3. A box contains 118 bags of marbles.
   There are eight marbles in each bag.
   How many marbles are there altogether?

4. 138 flowers are put equally into six vases.
   How many flowers are in each vase?

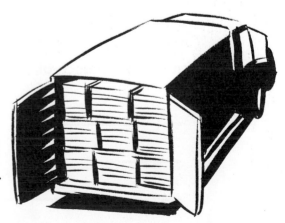

A
Write as a fraction the part of each shape that is shaded.

1.
2.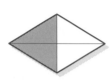
3.
4.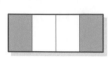

5.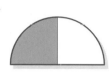
6.
7.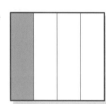
8.

B
Copy and complete.

1. $\frac{1}{2}$ of 18 = ☐
2. $\frac{1}{4}$ of 24 = ☐
3. $\frac{1}{4}$ of 32 = ☐
4. $\frac{1}{2}$ of 30 = ☐

5. $\frac{1}{4}$ of 20 = ☐
6. $\frac{1}{2}$ of 34 = ☐
7. $\frac{1}{4}$ of 28 = ☐
8. $\frac{1}{2}$ of 16 = ☐

C
Find a half of each of these figures.
Write the answers.

1.  64p
2. 34 g
3. 40 ml
4. 72p
5. 56 g
6. 86 ml

D
Find a quarter of each of these.
Write the answers.

1. 52 g
2. 80p
3. 68 ml
4. 92 g
5. 56p
6. 96 ml

E
Write a half of each of
these lengths.

1. _____

2. _____

3. _____

4. _____

Write a quarter of each of
these lengths.

1. _____

2. _____

3. _____

4. _____

Write as a fraction the part of each shape that is shaded.

1.
2.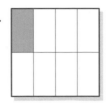
3.
4.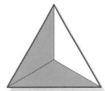

5.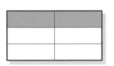
6.
7.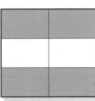
8.

B

Copy and complete.

1. $\frac{1}{5}$ of 25 = ☐   2. $\frac{1}{3}$ of 27 = ☐   3. $\frac{1}{6}$ of 36 = ☐   4. $\frac{1}{5}$ of 10 = ☐

5. $\frac{1}{3}$ of 15 = ☐   6. $\frac{1}{6}$ of 12 = ☐   7. $\frac{1}{5}$ of 15 = ☐   8. $\frac{1}{3}$ of 21 = ☐

C

Find $\frac{1}{3}$ of each of these.
Write the answers.

1. 39p
2. 15 litres
3. 45 g
4. £2.10
5. 63 cm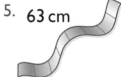

D

Find $\frac{1}{5}$ of each of these.
Write the answers.

1. 95 cm
2. £4.50
3. 35 litres
4. 65 g
5. 75p

E

Find $\frac{1}{6}$ of each of these.
Write the answers.

1. 42 g
2. 60p
3.  48 ml
4. 72 cm
5. £1.20

Copy and complete these fractions.

1.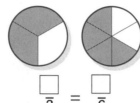

$$\frac{2}{\Box} = \frac{1}{2}$$

2.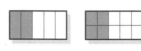

$$\frac{2}{5} = \frac{\Box}{10}$$

3.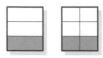

$$\frac{1}{3} = \frac{\Box}{6}$$

4.

$$\frac{\Box}{4} = \frac{\Box}{8}$$

5.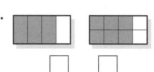

$$\frac{\Box}{3} = \frac{\Box}{6}$$

6.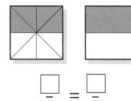

$$\frac{\Box}{\Box} = \frac{\Box}{\Box}$$

B Write which fraction is the smaller in each of these pairs.

1. $\frac{3}{4}$ or $\frac{1}{2}$ 2. $\frac{2}{3}$ or $\frac{5}{6}$ 3. $\frac{1}{5}$ or $\frac{3}{10}$ 4. $\frac{1}{2}$ or $\frac{3}{8}$

C Write which fraction is the bigger in each of these pairs.

1. $\frac{4}{5}$ or $\frac{7}{10}$ 2. $\frac{1}{3}$ or $\frac{3}{12}$ 3. $\frac{3}{4}$ or $\frac{7}{8}$ 4. $\frac{1}{6}$ or $\frac{1}{12}$

D Copy and complete these fractions.

1.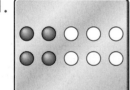

$$\frac{4}{10} = \frac{\Box}{5}$$

2.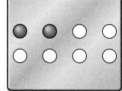

$$\frac{\Box}{8} = \frac{\Box}{4}$$

3.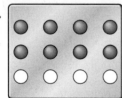

$$\frac{8}{\Box} = \frac{\Box}{3}$$

4.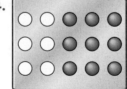

$$\frac{9}{\Box} = \frac{\Box}{5}$$

In a car park the colours of the cars were recorded.
Copy and complete these sentences,
writing the colours of the cars.

Car colour	Number
red	8
white	6
black	4
blue	3
green	2
silver	1
Total	24

1. $\frac{1}{4}$ of the cars were _____ .

2. $\frac{1}{6}$ of the cars were _____ .

3. $\frac{1}{3}$ of the cars were _____ .

4. $\frac{1}{12}$ of the cars were _____ .

5. $\frac{1}{8}$ of the cars were _____ .

6. $\frac{1}{24}$ of the cars were _____ .

Write the answers for these sums.

1. $\frac{1}{5}$ of 45

2. $\frac{1}{3}$ of 18

3. $\frac{1}{2}$ of 90

4. $\frac{1}{10}$ of 70

5. $\frac{1}{7}$ of 49

6. $\frac{1}{4}$ of 28

A traffic survey was carried out.

1. What is the total number of vehicles?
2. Write the number of each type of vehicle as a
   fraction of the total.

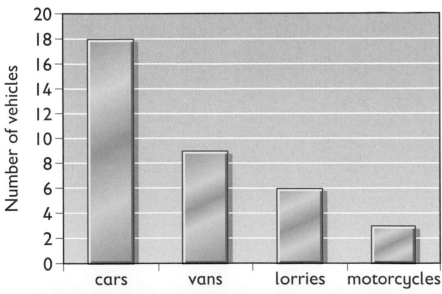

A Write the answers to these.

1. $\frac{1}{4}$ of 12
   $\frac{3}{4}$ of 12

2. $\frac{1}{3}$ of 6
   $\frac{2}{3}$ of 6

3. $\frac{1}{5}$ of 15
   $\frac{3}{5}$ of 15

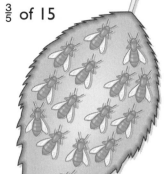

B Write your answers to these.

1. $\frac{3}{4}$ of 20
2. $\frac{2}{5}$ of 10
3. $\frac{3}{10}$ of 60
4. $\frac{5}{8}$ of 16
5. $\frac{2}{9}$ of 18
6. $\frac{4}{5}$ of 25
7. $\frac{2}{3}$ of 18
8. $\frac{5}{6}$ of 24

C What is the value of the following?

1. $\frac{3}{4}$ of £1·20
2. $\frac{2}{3}$ of £9
3. $\frac{3}{5}$ of £4·50
4. $\frac{9}{10}$ of £4
5. $\frac{2}{5}$ of £3·55
6. $\frac{5}{6}$ of £3·60

D Write $\frac{3}{4}$ of each of these numbers. | Write $\frac{2}{3}$ of each of these numbers.

1. 24
2. 44
3. 32

7. 27
8. 39
9. 60

4. 80
5. 56
6. 64

10. 36
11. 72
12. 84

Copy and complete these statements.

1. $\frac{1}{4}$ m = ☐ cm

2. $\frac{1}{2}$ kg = ☐ g

3. $\frac{3}{4}$ litre = ☐ ml

4. $\frac{1}{2}$ cm = ☐ mm

5. $\frac{1}{4}$ hour = ☐ minutes

6. $\frac{3}{4}$ kg = ☐ g

B

How many millilitres of water are there in each of these flasks?
Write your answers.

1. 4 l / 3 l / 2 l / 1 l

2. 2 l / 1 l

3. 3 l / 2 l / 1 l

4. $1\frac{1}{2}$ l / 1 l / $\frac{1}{2}$ l

5. $\frac{1}{2}$ l

C

Write your answers to these.

1. $\frac{4}{5}$ of 35 cm

2. $\frac{3}{5}$ of 155 mm

3. $\frac{2}{3}$ of 180 g

4. $\frac{3}{10}$ of 90 l

5. $\frac{5}{8}$ of 16 kg

6. $\frac{9}{10}$ of 120 ml

D

Find $\frac{3}{4}$ of these lengths.
Write them in centimetres.

1. 2 m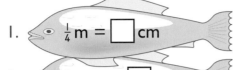

2. 1 m 60 cm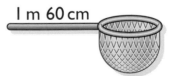

3. 2 m 24 cm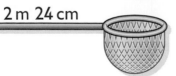

4. 3 m 20 cm

Copy and complete the following sums.

1. 2 · 9
    + 1 · 4
    _____

2. 3 · 7
    + 4 · 6
    _____

3. 1 3 · 8
    +   4 · 2
    _____

4.   6 · 9
    + 2 2 · 3
    _____

5. 3 1 · 6
    + 2 7 · 4
    _____

6. 2 9 · 9
    + 1 4 · 7
    _____

7.   8 · 4
    + 3 8 · 9
    _____

8. 4 7 · 2
    + 2 9 · 8
    _____

B

Sort these numbers into pairs that total 25. Write your answers.

 14.7 20.4 12.8 15.6 4.6 10.3 9.4 12.2

C

Write these totals.

1. 7·9 + 4·8   2. 6·3 + 19·5   3. 28·7 + 14·4   4. 19·6 + 17·9
5. 8·3 + 19·4 + 6·9   6. 9·2 + 27·8 + 13·6   7. 19·2 + 13·7 + 14·9

D

Write what numbers must be added to each of these to give an answer of 18?

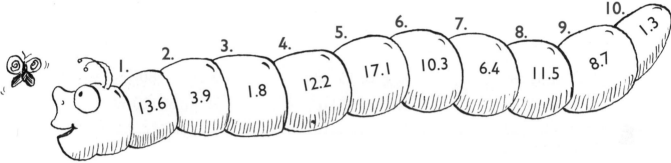

1. 13.6   2. 3.9   3. 1.8   4. 12.2   5. 17.1   6. 10.3   7. 6.4   8. 11.5   9. 8.7   10. 1.3

E

Write the answers to these sums.
Which is the odd one out?

1. 8.4 + 7.8   2. 3.9 + 12.3   3. 10.7 + 5.5

4. 9.6 + 6.6   5. 11.3 + 4.8   6. 8.1 + 8.1

A Write the answers to the sums.

1. 7·8
   − 4·3
   ____

2. 9·2
   − 5·1
   ____

3. 8·4
   − 3·9
   ____

4. 1 0·2
   − 7·8
   ____

5. 2 3·8
   − 1 1·9
   ____

6. 1 4·7
   −   8·9
   ____

7. 2 9·4
   − 1 9·9
   ____

8. 4 8·6
   − 1 9·7
   ____

B Subtract these numbers and write the answers.

1. 12·9 − 8·7   2. 28·4 − 13·9   3. 31·6 − 15·9   4. 27·2 − 18.4
5. 39·2 − 21·8   6. 42·1 − 21·2   7. 52·7 − 13·8   8. 31·7 − 20·8

C Sort these numbers into pairs that have a difference of 5·5.

18.3   23.2   18.1   13.4
12.6   7.9   23.8   17.7

D What must be subtracted from each of these to give an answer of 6?

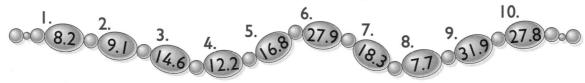

1. 8.2   2. 9.1   3. 14.6   4. 12.2   5. 16.8   6. 27.9   7. 18.3   8. 7.7   9. 31.9   10. 27.8

E Write the answers to these sums.
Which is the odd one out?

1. 19.6 − 13.7   2. 27.8 − 21.9   3. 20.6 − 14.7   4. 8.4 − 2.5

5. 46.9 − 41.0   6. 38.2 − 32.4   7. 72.1 − 66.2   8. 50.7 − 44.8

A Write the answers to these sums.

1.   3 · 4 7
     + 2 · 9 2
    _____

2.   6 · 8 4
     + 4 · 7 1
    _____

3.   8 · 2 9
     + 6 · 3 8
    _____

4.   1 2 · 9 6
     + 7 · 0 1
    _____

5.   1 7 · 5 8
     + 1 3 · 1 9
    _____

6.   2 3 · 1 9
     + 1 4 · 9 2
    _____

7.   3 1 · 8 9
     + 1 7 · 3 1
    _____

8.   3 7 · 9 2
     + 2 9 · 7 9
    _____

B Write the total cost for each of these shopping lists.

1. | Trainers
   | T-shirt
   | Swimsuit

2. | Socks
   | Tennis racquet
   | Basketball

3. | Basketball
   | Trainers
   | Socks

£5.08   £2.35   £9.99   £4.52   £31.25   £29.84

C Write what must be added to each of these to give an answer of 12.

1. 3.84
2. 9.11
3. 7.29
4. 6.48
5. 3.09
6. 10.61
7. 4.05
8. 11.12

D Find the missing digits.
Copy and complete the sums.

1.   ⬤ · 3 1
     + 7 · 2 9
    _____
     1 5 · 6 0

2.   1 9 · 8 ⬤
     + 1 3 · 2 9
    _____
     3 ⬤ · 1 6

3.   2 1 · ⬤ 4
     + 1 3 · 9 7
    _____
     ⬤ 5 · 0 ⬤

4.   3 ⬤ · 8 4
     + 1 6 · 9 ⬤
    _____
     5 6 · ⬤ 1

A

Find the difference in cost between the following pairs.

1. pen and ink
2. diary and paper
3. glue and scissors
4. diary and pen
5. paper and scissors
6. glue and ink

£2.14 £5.29 £1.76 £6.95 £2.47 £1.89

INK

glue stick

B

Write the change you would get from £10 if you bought each of these.

1. diary   2. paper   3. glue   4. pen   5. scissors   6. ink

C

Write the answers to these sums.

1.	2.	3.	4.
19·53 − 13·17	41·83 − 10·78	37·18 − 13·79	51·62 − 27·59

5.	6.	7.	8.
46·91 − 27·96	39·42 − 18·59	53·15 − 28·38	62·04 − 27·39

D

Write the answers to these sums.
Which is the odd one out?

1. 28.48 − 22.98
2. 23.43 − 16.83
3. 30.61 − 27.21

4. 38.74 − 31.04
5. 24.21 − 14.31
6. 21.47 − 12.67

These are some of the world's smallest mammals.

Mammal	Weight (g)	Length (cm)
Kitti's hognosed bat	2·1 g	2·9 cm
Pygmy shrew	1·5 g	3·6 cm
Pipistrelle bat	3·0 g	4·0 cm
Little brown bat	8·1 g	4·2 cm
Masked shrew	2·4 g	4·5 cm
Harvest mouse	4·9 g	5·8 cm

 A Write the difference in weight between the following pairs.

1. Pygmy shrew and Masked shrew.

2. Little brown bat and Pipistrelle bat.

3. Kitti's hognosed bat and Harvest mouse.

4. Pygmy shrew and Harvest mouse.

 B Write the difference in length between the following pairs.

1. Kitti's hognosed bat and Masked shrew.

2. Pygmy shrew and Pipistrelle bat.

3. Little brown bat and Harvest mouse.

4. Masked shrew and Pygmy shrew.

 C Write the total weight of each group of three mammals.

1. Pipistrelle bat
   Little brown bat
   Kitti's hognosed bat

2. Pygmy shrew
   Masked shrew
   Harvest mouse

3. Little brown bat
   Harvest mouse
   Pipistrelle bat

A These are the heights of six trees planted in a park.

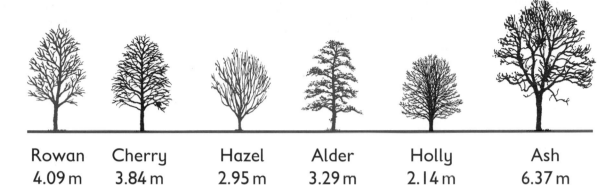

Rowan	Cherry	Hazel	Alder	Holly	Ash
4.09 m	3.84 m	2.95 m	3.29 m	2.14 m	6.37 m

1. Write the trees in order of height, starting with the shortest.
2. How much taller is the ash than each of the other trees?

 B Write what is the difference in height between:

1. the cherry and the holly;　　　2. the hazel and the alder;
3. the rowan and the cherry;　　　4. the alder and the holly.

 C This table shows by how much the trees have grown.

1. Write the new height of each of the trees.
2. Write which trees are now over 4 m in height.

Tree	Height	Growth
Rowan	4·09 m	58 cm
Cherry	3·84 m	42 cm
Hazel	2·95 m	39 cm
Alder	3·29 m	46 cm
Holly	2·14 m	37 cm
Ash	6·37 m	73 cm

D Use the new heights to find the difference between:

1. the cherry and the holly;　　　2. the hazel and the alder;
3. the rowan and the cherry;　　　4. the alder and the holly.

A

Answer the following questions.

1. Find the total of these numbers.
2. What must be added to the total to make 10 000?
3. What is the mean average of these numbers?
4. Which of the numbers can be divided exactly by 4?
5. Find $\frac{3}{4}$ of the largest number.
6. Find $\frac{2}{5}$ of the smallest number.
7. What is the difference between the largest and smallest numbers?

B

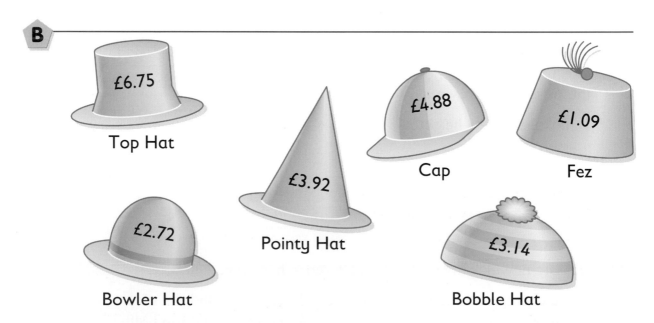

Write your answers to the following questions.
1. What is the total of these amounts?
2. Which hat is nearest to the mean average price?
3. What is the difference in price between the most and least expensive?
4. Which price is £2·28 less than £5?
5. What would be the total cost of three top hats and four bowler hats?
6. What would be the total cost of four pointy hats and two fezzes?

A Fruit and vegetables are being sold in boxes of six.

Write the price of the following items.

1. one leek
2. one courgette
3. one apple
4. one cabbage
5. one orange
6. one banana

B Write the difference in price between each of these pairs.

1. a leek and an apple
2. an orange and a banana
3. a cabbage and a courgette

C
1. Write the total price of one of each item.
2. Write the mean average price of the items.
3. Write which item is nearest in price to the mean average.

D Write how much change from £20 you would get for the following.

1.

3 courgettes

2 bananas

4 leeks

2.

2 oranges

4 cabbages

1 apple

3.

5 courgettes

2 cabbages

3 bananas

Answer the following questions.

1. What is the difference in length between the longest rope and the shortest?
2. What is the mean average length of the ropes?
3. Which rope is of average length?
4. Which rope can be cut into equal lengths of 15 cm?

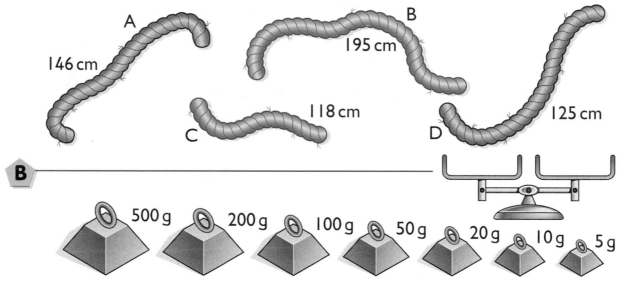

A 146 cm
B 195 cm
C 118 cm
D 125 cm

B

500 g 200 g 100 g 50 g 20 g 10 g 5 g

List the weights needed to balance each of these:

1. 530 g
2. 790 g
3. 475 g
4. 195 g

5. 1 kg 440 g
6. 4 kg 85 g
7. 8 kg 590 g
8. 7 kg 125 g

C

1. Match the labels to the containers.
2. If each of these amounts is doubled, what are the new amounts?
   Write your answers.

A   B   C

3 l   3 l   3 l
2 l   2 l   2 l
1 l   1 l   1 l

1 l 500 ml
1 l 250 ml
1 l 400 ml

A Use the train timetable to answer these questions.

1. How long does Train 2 take to travel from Cambridge to Letchworth?
2. If you need to be in Baldock for 8.00 pm, which train would you catch?
3. How long does Train 1 take to travel from Foxton to Ashwell?
4. If you arrived at Cambridge at 7.40 pm, how long would you have to wait for a train to Royston?
5. Has Train 3 arrived in Letchworth when Train 4 leaves Cambridge?
6. If Train 3 is 12 minutes late, what time will it arrive in Ashwell?

Train number:	1	2	3	4
Cambridge	1828	1906	1928	2002
Foxton	1837	1915	1937	2011
Shepreth	1839	1917	1939	2013
Meldreth	1842	1920	1942	2016
Royston	1846	1924	1946	2020
Ashwell	1851	1929	1951	2025
Baldock	1856	1934	1956	2030
Letchworth	1859	1937	1959	2033

B Write these times as 24 hour clock times.

1. 11.45 pm   2. 12.14 am   3. 1.35 pm
4. 6.32 am   5. 8.27 pm   6. 2.43 pm
7. 8.52 am   8. 9.11 pm   9. 12.34 pm

C Write these times as am or pm times.

1. 20.45   2. 08.33   3. 22.58
4. 17.25   5. 04.08   6. 10.09
7. 13.41   8. 15.49   9. 00.18

Answer each set of questions as quickly as you can.
Only write the answers.

A
1. 14 + 9
2. 23 + 8
3. 7 + 16
4. 14 + 18
5. 23 + 9
6. 8 + 14
7. 16 + 21
8. 27 + 11
9. 9 + 28
10. 18 + 17

B
1. 19 + 19
2. 17 + 23
3. 8 + 14
4. 17 + 7
5. 21 + 16
6. 14 + 28
7. 29 + 18
8. 26 + 12
9. 21 + 11
10. 28 + 24

C
1. 36 + 28
2. 39 + 17
3. 14 + 31
4. 27 + 42
5. 38 + 46
6. 32 + 42
7. 21 + 39
8. 46 + 17
9. 27 + 47
10. 31 + 39

D
1. 23 − 17
2. 18 − 9
3. 22 − 13
4. 17 − 4
5. 21 − 13
6. 28 − 18
7. 27 − 21
8. 22 − 14
9. 19 − 11
10. 28 − 13

E
1. 38 − 21
2. 36 − 14
3. 27 − 19
4. 18 − 9
5. 38 − 17
6. 29 − 13
7. 39 − 28
8. 34 − 25
9. 37 − 14
10. 30 − 19

F
1. 49 − 16
2. 42 − 19
3. 37 − 24
4. 39 − 17
5. 42 − 28
6. 46 − 37
7. 41 − 19
8. 37 − 21
9. 28 − 14
10. 48 − 19

Answer each set of questions as quickly as you can.
Only write the answers.

A
1. 4×6
2. 3×4
3. 6×2
4. 8×5
5. 9×3
6. 7×9
7. 4×4
8. 5×9
9. 6×6
10. 8×4

B
1. 5×2
2. 8×7
3. 9×6
4. 3×3
5. 2×9
6. 8×8
7. 3×8
8. 5×4
9. 9×9
10. 6×2

C
1. 7×7
2. 4×8
3. 6×7
4. 2×4
5. 8×3
6. 0×6
7. 7×4
8. 10×8
9. 6×3
10. 4×9

D
1. 8×8
2. 3×7
3. 4×10
4. 7×8
5. 9×3
6. 4×7
7. 6×8
8. 3×3
9. 5×10
10. 7×2

E
1. 6×8
2. 3×2
3. 0×4
4. 7×6
5. 3×9
6. 8×1
7. 9×8
8. 8×5
9. 6×4
10. 7×9

F
1. 3×5
2. 7×2
3. 8×8
4. 6×5
5. 5×7
6. 9×2
7. 6×7
8. 4×4
9. 8×2
10. 7×4

Answer each set of questions as quickly as you can.
Only write the answers.

A
1. $18 \div 2$
2. $27 \div 9$
3. $24 \div 6$
4. $45 \div 5$
5. $56 \div 8$
6. $72 \div 9$
7. $100 \div 10$
8. $14 \div 7$
9. $25 \div 5$
10. $80 \div 10$

B
1. $21 \div 7$
2. $16 \div 4$
3. $36 \div 9$
4. $42 \div 7$
5. $12 \div 6$
6. $18 \div 3$
7. $56 \div 7$
8. $24 \div 6$
9. $30 \div 5$
10. $50 \div 10$

C
1. $42 \div 6$
2. $12 \div 2$
3. $15 \div 3$
4. $28 \div 7$
5. $21 \div 3$
6. $14 \div 2$
7. $60 \div 6$
8. $27 \div 3$
9. $15 \div 5$
10. $32 \div 8$

D
1. $35 \div 7$
2. $90 \div 9$
3. $32 \div 4$
4. $8 \div 4$
5. $14 \div 7$
6. $18 \div 6$
7. $36 \div 4$
8. $48 \div 6$
9. $70 \div 10$
10. $15 \div 5$

E
1. $27 \div 9$
2. $81 \div 9$
3. $14 \div 2$
4. $28 \div 7$
5. $30 \div 3$
6. $20 \div 4$
7. $32 \div 8$
8. $24 \div 4$
9. $56 \div 7$
10. $18 \div 9$

F
1. $64 \div 8$
2. $12 \div 6$
3. $24 \div 3$
4. $9 \div 3$
5. $36 \div 6$
6. $72 \div 8$
7. $16 \div 8$
8. $28 \div 4$
9. $45 \div 9$
10. $27 \div 3$